CYCLE A

BUILDING FAMILY FAITH THROUGH LENT

LISA M. BELLECCI-ST.ROMAIN

LIGUORI PUBLICATIONS
ONE LIGUORI DRIVE
LIGUORI, MO 63057-9999
(314) 464-2500

Imprimi Potest:
James Shea, C.SS.R.
Provincial, St. Louis Province
The Redemptorists

Imprimatur:
+ Edward J. O'Donnell, D.D.
Archdiocesan Administrator, Archdiocese of St. Louis

ISBN 0-89243-807-X
Library of Congress Catalog Card Number: 95-80151

Printed in the United States of America
9 8 7 6 5 4 3 2
First Printing

Cover and interior art by Chris Sharp

Calendar

Page	Sunday or Feast	1996	1999	2002
9	1st Sun. of Lent	25 Feb.	21 Feb.	17 Feb.
11	2nd Sun. of Lent	3 Mar.	28 Feb.	24 Feb.
13	3rd Sun. of Lent	10 Mar.	7 Mar.	3 Mar.
18	4th Sun. of Lent	17 Mar.	14 Mar.	10 Mar.
20	5th Sun. of Lent	24 Mar	21 Mar.	17 Mar.
23	Passion Sunday	31 Mar.	28 Mar.	24 Mar.
29	Easter Sunday	7 Apr.	4 Apr.	31 Mar.

Introduction

HAVE YOU WISHED for a book that could help you share your faith with your children, a book that does not bore them or become tedious for you?

This book is that book! It gives your family a chance to share and think, while having fun with one another. As a family, you can study the Sunday Scriptures to make them come alive for your children. (Some weeks cite only a portion of the entire reading.) How you use the questions for reflection depends on the ages of your children or their desire to consider the issues. Use your judgment; see what works each week and what feels complete.

Each session is designed to last about fifteen

minutes, but there might be times when a good discussion keeps the session going longer. Some sessions require additional time and effort on the part of the leader.

All sessions end with a "treat" (suggestions provided). Sugar-free dietary needs have been considered, and many suggestions are available in both sugar and nonsugar forms. If you don't find the treat appropriate, choose something else. Enjoy your treat around the table or in the family meeting place to reinforce a sense of family unity.

The items needed for each session are generally those found around the house; options, however, are provided. The leader has the responsibility of gathering the items for his or her week and making any necessary advance preparations. Note: the leader need not always be a parent in the household. Grandparents or other relatives might like a turn, and older children can benefit from leading something fun, yet Scripture-oriented. The leader, however, should be old enough to take precautions around young children when materials and activities call for safety.

Set aside one special place in your house for your family's altar. It could be a corner table, the top of the television, the middle of the kitchen or dining-room table—anywhere your family decides. Each week the text will suggest placing something on the family altar space for the week. Thus, the space should not inconvenience family routine.

To accommodate family schedules, it's important to set aside a regular time to gather the family. Some families prefer to gather before Sunday liturgy to have an idea of what's coming up at church. Others gather the following week, to continue what they heard at church on Sunday. You decide what fits your family's schedule and preferences. With weekly regularity, growth and good times are guaranteed!

THE SEASON OF LENT

Theme: Faith is lived in the ordinary times of life.

Reading: *Matthew 4:1-11 (Gospel)*
Jesus was led into the desert by the Spirit to be tempted by the devil. He fasted forty days and forty nights, and afterward he was hungry. The tempter approached and said to him, "If you are the Son of God, command these stones to turn into bread." Jesus replied, "Scripture has it: 'Not on bread alone are we to live but on every utterance that comes from the mouth of God.'" Next, the devil took him to the Holy City, set him on the parapet of the temple, and said, "If you are the Son of God, throw yourself down. Scripture has it: 'God will bid the angels to take care of you; with their hands they will support you so that you may never stumble on a stone.'" Jesus answered, "Scripture also has it: 'You shall not put the Lord your God to the test.'" The devil then took him to a lofty mountain peak and displayed before him all the countries of the world in their magnificence, promising, "All of these I will bestow on you if you prostrate yourself in homage before me." At this, Jesus said to him, "Away with you, Satan! Scripture says: 'You shall do homage to the Lord your God, who alone shall you adore.'" At that the devil left him, and angels came and waited on him.

Materials: ✓ postcards of big cities or spectacular places (or pictures from a book or magazine) ✓ a picture of your house or a sheet of paper with your address written on it

Treat: plain toast (Have butter, jelly, marmalade, and other toppings available.)

Leader's Instructions: Gather the family, and open with prayer. Put the pictures and/or cards in the center of the group, read the Scripture, and lead the Share and Commit sections.

Share: In the reading, we hear about Jesus refusing the extraordinary, the spectacular. Sometimes there are boring or ordinary times in our lives; faith in Jesus and following Jesus does not mean it will always be exciting or spectacular.

Do you tend to get restless if nothing exciting is going on? Are you waiting for a miracle to truly give your heart to God? Are there some unspectacular things in your life you wish God would change? Do the unspectacular things cause you to doubt God's love for you just as you are, right now? How would you finish the sentence "I'll be okay when..."?

Does that give you a clue as to your dissatisfaction with the ordinary? What might you do instead? How can family members help you appreciate the ordinary and small wonders of life?

Commit: Each day this week, let's spend time noticing ordinary things: walking, baking, cleaning, talking, working. Let's be especially aware of how God loves us in those ordinary moments.

Altar Sign: Place the picture of your house or the card with your address on the altar space. Let it remind you to live and love in the ordinariness of life.

Prayer: God of day and night, summer and winter, season after season, we thank you for the routines of our lives that give stability. We ask your blessing on those times when we are restless. We pray for the grace to rest in you and your world. Amen.

Close: Hug each family member, and share the treat.

Second Sunday of Lent

Theme: God transfigures us.

Reading: *Matthew 17:1-3, 5-9 (Gospel)*
Jesus took Peter, James, and his brother John and led them up on a high mountain by themselves. He was transfigured before their eyes. His face became as dazzling as the sun, his clothes as radiant as light. Suddenly, Moses and Elijah appeared to them conversing with him and a bright cloud overshadowed them. Out of the cloud came a voice which said, "This is my beloved Son on whom my favor rests. Listen to him." When the disciples heard this, they fell forward on the ground, overcome with fear. Jesus came toward them and laying his hand on them, said, "Get up! Do not be afraid." When they looked up they did not see anyone but Jesus. As they were

coming down the mountainside, Jesus commanded them, "Do not tell anyone of the vision until the Son of Man rises from the dead."

Materials: ✓ mirrors, small enough to be held in one's hand

Treat: nut bread

Leader's Instructions: Gather the family, and place the mirrors in the center of the group. Open with prayer. Before you read the Scripture, explain that last week's reading was about Jesus resisting temptation to do the spectacular. Remind the family that Jesus was content to trust God in the ordinary. Explain that this week's reading tells about the Transfiguration of Jesus—definitely spectacular! After you read the Scripture, lead the Share and Commit sections.

Share: When you look in the mirror at yourself, what is your first thought or reaction? Many people in our society believe that they are not good enough because they compare themselves to an ideal of looks or popularity or amount of money earned.

How do people who don't think they're good enough act? Would a person who felt secure in God's love behave differently? How?

Have you ever seen someone who was "transformed" because of love? How do we let others know that they are loved? Would you like the family to do something special that lets you know you are loved? What?

Commit: This week, let's smile at ourselves every time we look in a mirror. At that moment, let's thank God for loving us.

Altar Sign: Place one of the small hand-held mirrors on the altar space. Each time you pass it this week, pause and smile and know that God smiles with you.

Prayer: Dear God, your image of who we are and what we can be is sometimes hidden to us. We pray for the grace to see ourselves as you see us, that we might be secure as we do your work here on earth. Amen.

Close: Share a hug, and enjoy the treat.

Third Sunday of Lent

Theme: Jesus desires to give eternal life.

Reading: *John 4:5-15,19-26,39, 40-42 (Gospel)*
Jesus had to pass through Samaria, and his journey brought him to a Samaritan town named Sychar near the plot of land that Jacob had given to his son Joseph. This was the site of Jacob's well. Jesus, tired from his journey, sat down at the well. The hour was about noon.

When a Samaritan woman came to draw water, Jesus said to her, "Give me a drink." (His disciples had gone off into town to buy provisions.) The Samaritan woman said to him, "You are a Jew. How can you ask me, a Samaritan and a woman, for a drink?" (Recall that Jews have nothing to do with Samaritans.) Jesus replied: "If only you recognized God's gift, and who it is that is asking you for a drink, you would have asked him instead, and he would have given you living water." "Sir," she challenged him, "you don't have a bucket and this well is deep. Where do you expect to get this flowing water? Surely, you don't pretend to be greater than our ancestor Jacob, who gave us this well and drank from it with his family and flocks?" Jesus replied: "Everyone who drinks this water will be thirsty again. But whoever drinks the water I give will never be thirsty; no, the water I give shall become a fountain within, leaping up to provide eternal life."

The woman said to him, "Give me this water, sir, so that I won't grow thirsty and have to keep coming here to draw water. I can see you are a prophet. Our ancestors worshiped on this mountain, but you people claim that Jerusalem is the place where all ought to worship God." Jesus told her, "Believe me, woman, an hour is coming when you will worship God neither on this mountain nor in Jerusalem. An hour is coming, and is already here, when authentic worshipers will worship God in Spirit and truth. Indeed, it is just such worshipers that God seeks. God is Spirit, and those who worship must worship in Spirit and truth." The woman said to him: "I know there is a Messiah coming. When he comes, he will tell us everything." Jesus replied, "I who speak to you am he."

Many Samaritans from that town believed in him on the strength of the woman's word of testimony: "He told me everything I ever did." The result was that, when these Samaritans came to him, they begged him to stay with them awhile. So Jesus stayed there two days, and through his own spoken word many more came to faith. As they told the woman, "No longer does our faith depend on your story. We have heard for ourselves, and we know that this really is the Savior of the world."

Materials: ✓ pencils ✓ scissors ✓ construction paper or poster board ✓ crayons or markers ✓ pieces of clay (Copy the outlines of the figures on pages 15 and 16 onto the construction paper or poster board. Cut them out and color the figures as you like, or let family

Disciples

Jesus

Samaritan woman

Samaritan townspeople

members color them before the Scripture reading. In order to move them around easily during the reading, place the bottom of each figure in a one-inch ball of clay, flattened at the bottom.)

Treat: gingerbread people, one per person

Leader's Instructions: Gather the family, and open with prayer. As you read the Scripture, have two or more people move the figures around to "act out" the story. Lead the Share and Commit sections.

Share: Which one of the characters in the story is spiritually like you? In what way? Have you been spiritually like one of the other people? Are you satisfied with how you "spiritually" are now? If you were at the well with Jesus today, what would you talk to him about? What do you think he would say to you?

Commit: This week, let's meet Jesus at the well in our imagination. Let's talk with him and listen to what he has to say to us.

Altar Sign: Place the figures from the story on the altar space as a reminder to talk to Jesus now, just as you are.

Prayer: Dear God, you are always willing to come and meet us where we are. We thank you for this and we pray for the grace to respond to you with our whole selves. Amen.

Close: Have a glass of water with your treat, and share a family hug.

Theme: Seeing faith truths requires more than physical vision.

Reading: *John 9:1, 6-9, 13-17, 34-38 (Gospel)*
As Jesus walked along, he saw a man who had been blind from birth. With that, Jesus spat on the ground, made mud with his saliva, and smeared the man's eyes with the mud. Then Jesus told him, "Go wash in the pool of Siloam." So the man went off and washed and came back able to see. His neighbors and the people who had been accustomed to seeing him beg began to ask, "Isn't this the fellow who used to sit and beg?" Some were claiming it was he; others maintained it was not but someone who looked like him. The man himself said, "I'm the one, all right."

They took the man who had been born blind to the Pharisees. (Note that it was on a sabbath that Jesus had made the mud paste and opened his eyes.) The Pharisees, in turn, began to inquire how he had recovered his sight. He told them. "He put mud on my eyes. I washed it off, and now I can see." This prompted some of the Pharisees to assert, "This man cannot be from God because he does not keep the sabbath." Others objected, "If one is a sinner, how could that one perform signs like these?" They were sharply divided over him. Then they addressed the blind man again: "Since it was your eyes he opened, what do you have to say about him?" "He is a prophet," he replied. "What!" they exclaimed. "You are steeped in sin from your birth and you are giving us lectures?" With that, they threw him out bodily.

When Jesus heard of his expulsion, he sought him out and asked him, "Do you believe in the Son of Man?" He answered, "Who is he, sir, that I may believe in him?" "You have seen him," Jesus replied. "He is speaking to you now." "I do believe, Lord," he said, and bowed down to worship him.

Materials: ✓ three scarves or similar material (long enough to use as a blindfold)

Treat: a layered treat (for example, double-dipped cone or sandwich cookies)

Leader's Instructions: Gather the family members, open with prayer, and ask for a volunteer to be blindfolded. Explain to the person that he or she will have to remain patient throughout the Scripture reading. Tie the scarves around the person's eyes, creating three layers of darkness. (Be sure the person can breathe.) Begin reading the Scripture. When you read the part about the man washing off the mud and being able to see, have someone remove the outermost scarf from the blindfolded person. When you read the part about the man stating that Jesus is a prophet, have someone remove the next scarf. When you read the final statement, "I do believe, Lord," have the final scarf removed. Lead the Share and Commit sections.

Share: Why didn't all three scarves come off when the blind man was able to see? What does this tell us about our faith life, even if we can see with our eyes? In what ways can we use all our senses and our other capabilities to increase our faith and that of others?

How can we help one another do this?

Jesus broke the law of not working on the sabbath. When might it be okay to ignore a law as Jesus did?

Commit: This week, let's use one of our senses each day to increase our own faith or that of another person.

Altar Sign: Place the three scarves on the altar space to remind the family of the constant unwrapping that is involved in spiritual seeing and growing.

Prayer: O God, our creator, you made us with so much potential and with so many abilities. Help us use what we have in a way that increases our faith. We pray for the grace to know how you need us to do this. Amen.

Close: Share a hug and the treat.

Fifth Sunday of Lent

Theme: Faith in Jesus unbinds us.

Reading: *John 11:3-7, 17, 20-27, 33-45 (Gospel)*
Two sisters sent word to Jesus to inform him, "Lord, the one you love is sick." Upon hearing this, Jesus said: "This sickness is not to

end in death; rather it is for God's glory, that through it the Son of God may be glorified." Jesus loved Martha and her sister and Lazarus very much. Yet, after hearing that Lazarus was sick, he stayed on where he was for two days more. Finally, he said to his disciples, "Let us go back to Judea."

When Martha heard that Jesus was coming, she went to meet him, while Mary sat at home. Martha said to Jesus, "Lord, if you had been here, my brother would never have died. Even now, I am sure that God will give you whatever you ask." "Your bother will rise again," Jesus assured her. "I know he will rise again," Martha replied, "in the resurrection on the last day." Jesus told her, "I am the resurrection and the life: those who believe in me, though they die, will come to life; and those who are alive and believe in me will never die. Do you believe this?" "Yes, Lord," she replied. "I have come to believe that you are the Messiah, the Son of God: the one who is to come into the world."

When Jesus saw Mary weeping and the Jewish folk who had accompanied her out of the house also weeping, he was troubled in spirit, moved by the deepest emotions. "Where have you laid him?" Jesus asked. "Lord, come and see," they said. Jesus began to weep, which caused the Jews to remark, "See how much he loved him!" But some said, "He opened the eyes of that blind man. Why could he not have done something to stop this man from dying?"

Once again, troubled in spirit, Jesus approached the tomb. It was a cave with a stone laid across it. "Take away the stone," Jesus directed. Martha said to him, "Lord, it has been four days now; surely there will be a stench!" Jesus replied, "Did I not assure you that if you believed you would see the glory of God?" They then took away the stone, and Jesus looked upward and said, "Father, I thank you for having heard me. I know that you always hear me but I have said this for the sake of the crowd, that they may believe that you sent me." Having said this, he called loudly, "Lazarus, come out!" The dead man came out, bound hand and foot with linen strips, his face wrapped in a cloth. "Untie him," Jesus told them, "and let him go free." This caused many of the Jews who had come to visit Mary, and had seen what Jesus did, to put their faith in him.

Materials: ✓ 12- by 24-inch strips of cloth or gauze (one per person)

Treat: long strips of taffy or licorice

Leader's Instructions: Using the strips of cloth or gauze, wrap together all the fingers on each person's hands and/or wrap their legs together at the ankles. Do this twenty to thirty minutes before the meeting, and then ask the family to gather. After opening prayer, begin reading the Scripture. When you read the part about Jesus commanding Lazarus to be untied, direct family members to untie one another. Lead the Share and Commit sections.

Share: Why was it good for us to experience having our hands and feet tied? What are some ways people are not free within themselves?

What fears, worries, or memories keep you from being free to act as you believe Jesus would want you to act? How can we help one another attain freedom? If you have some hurt in your life about which, like Martha, you want to say to God, "If only you had...," would you be willing to forgive God and trust God again? How could someone help you do that?

Jesus said that he knew God always heard his prayers. How do you know when God has heard your prayers?

Commit: Every day this week, let's pray for the grace to be free of a particular worry, fear, or memory. Let's act on that as we feel led by God.

Altar Sign: Place the strips of cloth or gauze on the altar space to remind the family that they are set free by Christ. Encourage the family to pray by the altar space when they need the courage to be free from some fear.

Prayer: O God, your Son lived with us and knew how much we hurt. We pray that through him, you will set us free. We pray for the grace to be free and for the wisdom to know what to do. Amen.

Close: Share a hug and the treat.

Passion Sunday

(PALM SUNDAY)

Theme: Popularity doesn't last; faithfulness to God does.

Reading: *Matthew 21:1-11 (Gospel from the Procession)*
As the crowd drew near Jerusalem, entering Bethphage on the Mount of Olives, Jesus sent off two disciples with the instruction:

"Go into the village straight ahead of you and you will immediately find an ass and her colt tied there. Untie them and lead them back to me. If anyone says a word to you say, 'The master needs them.' Then he will let them go at once." This came about to fulfill what was said through the prophet: "Tell the daughter of Zion, your king comes to you without display astride an ass, astride a colt, the foal of a beast of burden."

So the disciples went off and did what Jesus had ordered; they brought the ass and the colt and laid their cloaks on them, and he mounted. The huge crowd spread their cloaks on the road, while some began to cut branches from the trees and laid them along his path. The groups preceding him as well as those following kept crying out: "God save the Son of David! Blessed be he who comes in the name of God! God save him from on high!" As Jesus entered Jerusalem the whole city was stirred to its depths, demanding, "Who is this?" And the crowd kept answering, "This is the prophet Jesus from Nazareth in Galilee."

Materials: ✓ one balloon ✓ palm branches

Treat: matzo crackers and apple slices

Leader's Instructions: Gather the family. After opening prayer, begin the reading. When you get to the part about the crowd cutting branches and crying out, blow up the balloon and tie it. As you finish the reading, hold the balloon and ask: "Will it stay blown up forever?" When someone responds "No," go on to explain that Jesus' popularity didn't last forever either. It was going to fade as people let themselves be pressured by some of the religious leaders and others around them. Then have the older children or other adults tell the story from the Last Supper to Jesus' burial, using the following events as guidelines: (1) the betrayer; (2) the Last Supper; (3) Peter's denial foretold; (4) the agony in the Garden; (5) Jesus arrested; (6) Jesus before the Sanhedrin; (7) Peter's denial; (8) Jesus handed over to Pilate; (9) Jesus before Pilate; (10) the crowning with thorns; (11) the way to the cross; (12) the Crucifixion; (13) the death of Jesus; (14) the burial of Jesus.

Share: How do you think the disciples of Jesus felt after the burial? We have the advantage today of knowing that he would rise again and is still with us. When you feel like the disciples did, for whatever reason, how will you remember that Jesus is risen and with you? What would you like the family to do for you at those times?

Have there been times when you were popular but lost that popularity? Looking back, do you notice a difference in your faith life during those times?

Commit: This week, let's support one another when we're feeling low. Let's be constant in faith despite rising or decreasing popularity. Let's attend services for the Easter Triduum—Holy Thursday, Good Friday, and Holy Saturday.

Altar Sign: Leave the balloon on the altar space as a reminder to be faithful to God no matter how popular it might or might not be.

Prayer: O God of heaven, you looked down and saw how people treated Jesus. We ask for the grace to be as faithful as he was when people mistreat us or misunderstand us. Amen.

Close: Share a hug, and enjoy your treat.

THE SEASON OF EASTER

Easter Sunday

(EASTER VIGIL)

Theme: Some things are too good to be true!

Reading: *Matthew 28:1-10 (Gospel)*

After the sabbath, as the first day of the week was dawning, Mary Magdalene and the other Mary came to see the tomb. And behold, there was a great earthquake; for an angel of the Lord descended from heaven, approached, rolled back the stone, and sat upon it. His appearance was like lightning and his clothing was white as snow. The guards were shaken with fear of him and became like the dead.

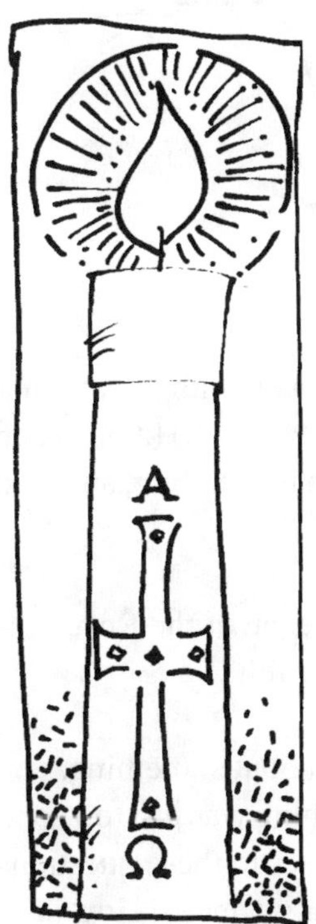

Then the angel said to the women in reply, "Do not be afraid! I know that you are seeking Jesus the crucified. He is not here, for he has been raised just as he said. Come and see the place where he lay. Then go quickly and tell the disciples, 'He has been raised from the dead, and he is going before you to Galilee; there you will see him.' Behold I have told you."

Then they went away quickly from the tomb, fearful yet overjoyed, and ran to announce this to the disciples. And behold, Jesus met them on their way and greeted them. They approached, embraced his feet, and did him homage. Then Jesus said to them, "Do not be afraid. Go tell my brothers and sisters to go to Galilee, and there they will see me."

Materials: ✓ white candle ✓ the word JOY cut out of white or yellow construction paper ✓ pencil ✓ dyed eggs (if your family does this tradition)

Treat: a family dessert that is extremely special

Leader's Instructions: Gather the family. Open with prayer, and read the Scripture. As you read the angel's words, "He has been raised from the dead," light the candle. Finish the reading, and lead the Share and Commit sections.

Share: Would you like to have been at the scene of the Resurrection? What would you have done, thought, or felt?

Have there been times when you felt so glad about something, you couldn't believe it? Did you ever think something was just too good to be true? (Ask someone to write the responses to these questions on the JOY letters.) What did you do with your gladness? How does it feel to remember it now? (Optional: How do these eggs we've dyed help us celebrate the joy of today?)

Commit: Let's take time each day this week to remember the joy of the people in the gospel and our joy at the "too-good-to-be-true" times. Let's remember this joy as we go about our days.

Altar Sign: Put the white candle on the altar space, and leave it there throughout the Easter season. Place the JOY letters next to it. (If you have dyed eggs, place them on the altar space as well.) Let the candle and the JOY letters remind you of the joy that is yours as you share in the victory of the risen Christ.

Prayer: God of joy and gladness, we thank you for the joy and life your Son, Jesus, has brought to us. We pray to live each day in that joy, no matter what might happen. We pray for the grace to bring joy to others. Amen.

Close: Hug one another, and enjoy your treat.

Also available...

Building Family Faith Through Lent
Cycle C
$2.95

Building Family Faith
Weekly Lectionary-Based Activities
Cycles A, B, & C
by Lisa Bellecci-st.romain

Includes weekly sharing and study sessions for each Church season (Advent, Christmas, Ordinary Time, Lent, and Easter). **$10.95 each**

More Lenten resources for the family from Liguori...

Lent Begins at Home
Family Prayers and Activities
by Pat and Rosemary Ryan

Help your whole family share the true meaning of Lent through Bible readings, collages, charitable acts, prayers, recipes, and more. **$2.95**

Lent Is for Children
Stories, Activities, Prayers
Revised and Expanded
by Julie Keleman

Imaginative ways to introduce children to Lenten basics such as fasting, temptation, and reconciliation. Now revised with new games and activities, children will discover not just the "how to" of Lenten practices but the "why" behind them. **$2.95**

Order from your local bookstore or write
Liguori Publications
Box 060, Liguori, MO 63057-9999
(Please add $2 for postage and handling to prepaid orders under $9.99; $3 for orders between $10 and $14.99; $4 for orders over $15.)